W9-BYB-494

THE MIAMI DOLPHINS

Sloan MacRae

PowerKiDS press.

New York

Published in 2011 by The Rosen Publishing Group, Inc.
29 East 21st Street, New York, NY 10010

Copyright © 2011 by The Rosen Publishing Group, Inc.

All rights reserved. No part of this book may be reproduced in any form without permission in writing from the publisher, except by a reviewer.

First Edition

Editor: Amelie von Zumbusch
Book Design: Greg Tucker
Layout Design: Julio Gil

Photo Credits: Cover (Dan Marino), p. 17 Peter Brouillet/Getty Images; cover (Jake Long), p. 21 G. Newman Lowrance/Getty Images; cover (Bob Griese), pp. 5, 22 (top) Vernon Biever/Getty Images; cover (background) Scott Boehm/Getty Images; pp. 7, 9, 22 (bottom) Al Messerschmidt/Getty Images; p. 11 John Vawter Collection/Diamond Images/Getty Images; pp. 13, 15 Focus on Sport/Getty Images; p. 19 Stan Honda/AFP/Getty Images.

Library of Congress Cataloging-in-Publication Data

MacRae, Sloan.
  The Miami Dolphins / by Sloan MacRae. — 1st ed.
      p. cm. — (America's greatest teams)
  Includes index.
  ISBN 978-1-4488-3167-8 (library binding) — ISBN 978-1-4488-3172-2 (pbk.) —
  ISBN 978-1-4488-3173-9 (6-pack)
  1. Miami Dolphins (Football team)—History—Juvenile literature. I. Title.
  GV956.M47M23 2011
  796.332'6409759381—dc22
                                2010037467

Manufactured in the United States of America

CPSIA Compliance Information: Batch #WW11PK: For Further Information contact Rosen Publishing, New York, New York at 1-800-237-9932

CONTENTS

PERFECT

Every sports team tries to be **perfect**. The last thing any sports player wants to do is lose a game. Losing games is part of sports, though. It happens sooner or later. The Miami Dolphins were the first team in the National Football League, or the NFL, to win every game in the regular season and the **postseason**. This gave them a perfect season. Other football teams came close, but the Dolphins were the first to win every game.

The Miami Dolphins have not been around for as long as some of the teams in the NFL. They have done a lot in a very short amount of time.

The 1972 Dolphins had many great players. One was quarterback Bob Griese, seen here in the Super Bowl that rounded out the team's perfect season.

NEAR THE BEACH

The city of Miami, Florida, is known for its beaches. When people visit the beaches there, they can often see dolphins swimming and playing in the ocean. This makes the Dolphins a great name for a football team from Miami.

All the teams in the NFL have **logos**. Logos help fans tell the teams apart. Some logos are just colorful letters that stand for different cities. The Dolphins' logo shows a dolphin wearing a football helmet. The helmet has an *M*, which stands for "Miami," on it. The Dolphins' colors are a shade of bluish green called aqua and a shade of orange called coral.

T. D. is the Dolphins' mascot. He wears a Dolphins helmet and uniform. T. D. runs around the field during games and makes fans laugh.

THE PHINS

The Dolphins play in a **stadium** called Sun Life Stadium. It is near Miami. Sun Life Stadium is also the home of the Orange Bowl. This is one of the biggest college football games of the year. Sun Life Stadium is famous for more than football. The Florida Marlins baseball team also plays there.

The Dolphins have one of the biggest fan bases in the NFL. Football fans sometimes call the team the Phins or the Fins for short. Some people call them the Fish. This nickname does not make a lot of sense, though. Dolphins are not fish. They are **mammals**, just like people!

These Dolphins fans are dressed up to root for their team. They are wearing the team colors. They even put on wigs and painted their faces!

A NAMING CONTEST

In the 1960s, an actor named Danny Thomas and a lawyer named Joe Robbie worked to bring a **professional** football team to Miami. Their hard work paid off. Miami got its team in 1965. The new team needed a name, though. The owners held a contest to name the team. Nearly 20,000 people wrote in with ideas. Some suggested names were the Suns or the Sharks. The Dolphins was the winning name.

Most new teams struggle in their first seasons. The Dolphins lost most of their games during the early years. Fans would not have to wait very long for a winning team, though.

In their second season, the Dolphins won 4 games and lost 10. On October 8, 1967, they lost the game seen here to the Kansas City Chiefs, 41–0.

THE 1970S AND THE PERFECT SEASON

In 1970, the Dolphins hired a new head **coach** named Don Shula. Shula had been a pretty good football player years earlier. He turned out to be an excellent coach. The Dolphins reached the **Super Bowl** at the end of the 1971 season. Sadly, they lost to the Dallas Cowboys.

Miami came back in 1972 and had the greatest season in NFL history. They did not lose one game. They even beat the Washington Redskins in the Super Bowl! They won the Super Bowl again the following season. Star players like Bob Griese and Larry Csonka made the Dolphins one of the best teams of the 1970s.

Along with big stars, the 1972 Dolphins team had great, but less famous, defensive players. They were called the No-Name Defense.

DAN MARINO

The Dolphins continued to shine in the 1980s. They made the postseason several times and played in two Super Bowls. A young **quarterback** named Dan Marino joined the team in 1983. Miami fans knew Marino was going to be good. They had no idea how good, though. Marino quickly became one of the best quarterbacks in the game.

Marino led the Dolphins to the Super Bowl in 1985. However, they lost to the San Francisco 49ers. Marino never reached the Super Bowl again. Even the greatest players do not always win Super Bowls.

Here, head coach Don Shula (left) talks to quarterbacks Don Strock (center) and Dan Marino (right) during a Dolphins game.

BREAKING RECORDS

The Dolphins did not reach the Super Bowl in the 1990s. They came close, though. They had some great seasons and often made the **play-offs**. Marino made football history in the 1990s by setting many NFL records. In 1995, he broke three of the most important quarterback records. He became the best passer yet in football history by reaching 48,841 passing yards, 352 touchdowns, and 3,913 completions, or passes that are caught.

Though he did not lead the Dolphins to another Super Bowl, Dolphins fans will always love Marino. They think he might be the greatest quarterback of all time. In early 2000, Marino retired. The Dolphins would need new heroes.

Marino was great at passing, or throwing the ball to other members of his team. He passed for 3,000 yards or more in 13 different seasons.

NEW LEADERS

The 2000 NFL season began with football fans wondering if the Dolphins could be good without Dan Marino. They were great! **Running back** Lamar Smith became a team leader. Miami had a very strong **defense** with great players such as Jason Taylor and Zach Thomas. The Dolphins reached the play-offs in the 2000 and 2001 seasons.

The Dolphins had good players during the rest of the 2000s. It takes more than good players to make a great football team, though. They needed great leaders. The Dolphins of these years were not a bad team. They did not have the success their fans remembered from years past, though.

Lamar Smith, left, played for the Dolphins in the 2000 and 2001 seasons. In 2000, he set a record by carrying the ball 40 times during a postseason game.

THE WILDCAT OFFENSE

The Dolphins still have what it takes to win Super Bowls. They struggled for part of the 2000s, but they came back in 2008. Miami hired a new coach named Tony Sparano. In his first season, Sparano used a plan called the wildcat **offense**. This allows the offense to move the ball down the field quickly. It makes it hard for other teams to stop them.

Miami has a smart coach. It also has good players, such as **offensive lineman** Jake Long and quarterbacks Chad Pennington and Chad Henne. The Miami Dolphins will have many more great seasons. Someday they may even have another perfect one.

Jake Long (center) started playing for the Dolphins in 2008. He quickly became one of the NFL's best offensive linemen.

MIAMI DOLPHINS TIMELINE

1965

The Miami Dolphins are formed.

1966

The Miami Dolphins play their first regular-season game. They lose to the Oakland Raiders.

1970

Don Shula becomes the head coach of the Dolphins.

1973

The Dolphins beat the Washington Redskins in the Super Bowl and become the first NFL team to record a perfect season.

1974

The Dolphins win their second Super Bowl by beating the Minnesota Vikings.

1980

Quarterback Bob Griese wins his hundredth game.

1983

The Dolphins pick Dan Marino in the NFL draft.

1984

Marino breaks the NFL record for most touchdown passes in a season.

2008

Tony Sparano becomes the head coach of the Dolphins.

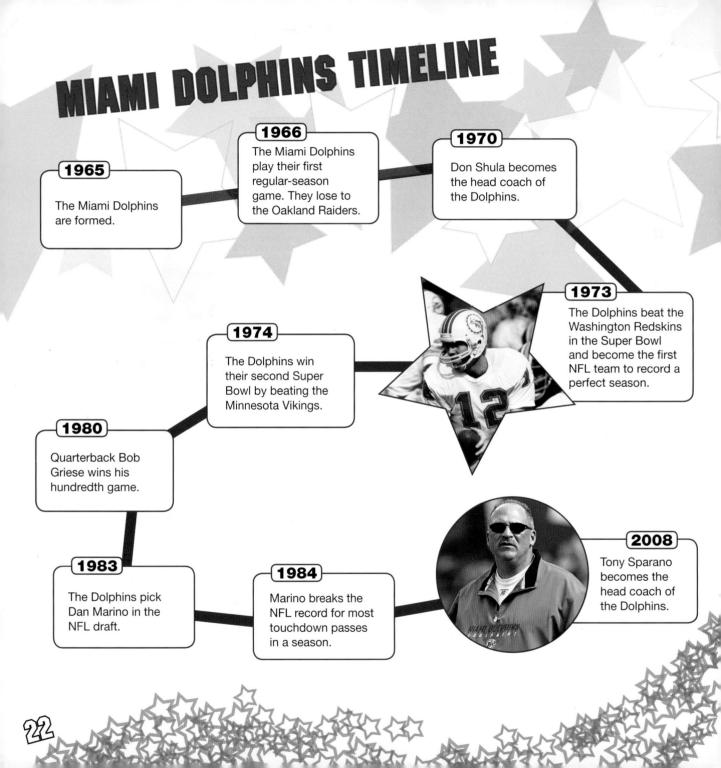

GLOSSARY

COACH (KOHCH) A person who directs a team.

DEFENSE (DEE-fents) When a team tries to stop the other team from scoring.

LOGOS (LOH-gohz) Pictures, words, or letters that stand for teams or companies.

MAMMALS (MA-mulz) Warm-blooded animals that have backbones and hair, breathe air, and feed milk to their young.

OFFENSE (O-fents) When a team tries to score points in a game.

OFFENSIVE LINEMAN (O-fent-siv LYN-mun) A member of a football team's offense whose biggest job is to block members of the other team's defense.

PERFECT (PER-fikt) Having nothing wrong.

PLAY-OFFS (PLAY-ofs) Games played after the regular season ends to see who will play in the championship game.

POSTSEASON (pohst-SEE-zun) Games played after the regular season.

PROFESSIONAL (pruh-FESH-nul) Having players who are paid.

QUARTERBACK (KWAHR-ter-bak) A football player who directs his team's plays.

RUNNING BACK (RUN-ing BAK) A football player whose job is to take or catch the ball and run with it.

STADIUM (STAY-dee-um) A place where sports are played.

SUPER BOWL (SOO-per BOHL) The championship game of NFL football.

INDEX

WEB SITES

Due to the changing nature of Internet links, PowerKids Press has developed an online list of Web sites related to the subject of this book. This site is updated regularly. Please use this link to access the list:
www.powerkidslinks.com/teams/fdolphins/